THE
BRITISH EMPIRE
IN COLOUR

THIS IS A CARLTON BOOK

Text copyright © 2002 Trans World International, Inc
Design copyright © 2002 Carlton Books Limited

This edition published by Carlton Books Limited 2002
20 Mortimer Street
London
W1T 3JW

A CIP catalogue record for this book is available
from the British Library.

ISBN 1 84222 517 0

Picture research: Joanne King
Editor: Claire Richardson
Cover design: Alison Tutton
Art direction: Vicky Holmes
Design: Peter Bailey
Production: Janette Davis

Printed in Italy

THE
BRITISH EMPIRE
IN COLOUR

STEWART BINNS

CARLTON
BOOKS

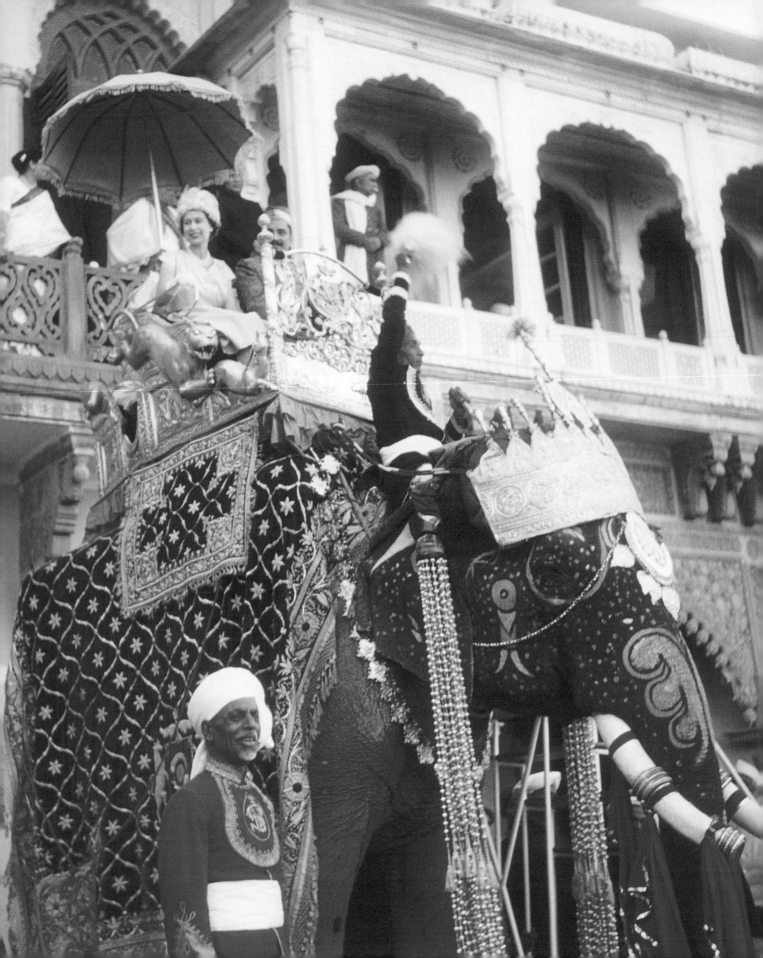

CONTENTS

1497–1815
INTRODUCTION

The history of the civilized world has, in large part, been a history of empires: Greek, Roman, Inca, Han, Islamic; each has left an indelible mark on the modern world. However, it is arguable that no empire has had a greater presence in history than the British Empire. It touched every continent and every major religion, held domain over hundreds of millions of people and played a significant part in shaping the destinies of at least three score of the world's nation states. Perhaps most significantly of all, it gave to the world the English language – the global *lingua franca* of commerce, entertainment, science and politics.

Many motives drove the British in the search for and conquest of their Empire. There were idealistic and altruistic intentions; there were materialistic and megalomanic imperatives; and there were patriots and zealots as well as healers and missionaries. Similarly, imperial rule had many faces: sometimes it was benign, often it was cruel; occasionally it was malicious usually it was patronising.

For the Empire's subjects there was little or no choice but to accept the governance of London. Many embraced it wholeheartedly, at least for a while; most put up with it as best they could. But, eventually, all but a few rejected it and rebelled against it.

It is not that the British Empire was a singular phenomenon. The British themselves were and are a multifaceted people, while their empire had as many varieties and complexions as it had islands, territories, dominions, colonies, protectorates and mandates.

From the mundane – like its street names and postboxes – to the magnificent – like its art and architecture – the legacy of the Empire will last for many generations. Britain changed forever the lands it ruled, but Britain was also changed irrevocably, as it moved from being the Anglo-Celtic imperial homeland of the world's most powerful empire, to a multicultural, decentralized middle-ranking nation, firmly anchored to its European neighbours.

Some authors would argue that the British Empire began when Henry II invaded Ireland in 1171, but Ireland is a vexing subject for historians of the Empire. For the greater part of the Empire's duration, the Irish served as the soldiers, colonizers and administrators, while, at the same time, being themselves ruled at home by the English. This paradox only resolved itself in 1922 with the creation of the Irish Free State. Of course, Britain itself is also a paradox, for there are many in Northern Ireland, Scotland and Wales who would see themselves as inappropriately and unacceptably ruled by the English. Whether this paradox will be resolved by the establishment of national parliaments in Belfast, Edinburgh and Cardiff remains to be seen. However, for the purpose of this book, the British, including their Irish subjects, will be regarded as acting in unison with respect to the Empire, while the history of Ireland will be left for others to contemplate.

Perhaps a less contentious claim for the beginning of the British Empire is the discovery and establishment of Newfoundland by John Cabot in 1497. However, Cabot was a Genoese adventurer (Giovanni Caboto) in the service of Henry VII and Newfoundland was not recognized as a colony until 1824. Nonetheless, by 1670 British explorers and merchants had established colonies in Virginia and Maryland, in Bermuda, Antigua, Barbados and Jamaica, and the Hudson's Bay Company was established in Canada. The East India Company had been trading in India since 1600 and the British slave trade had established settlements in West Africa. The second half of the eighteenth century was vital to the growing power of the British Empire. Robert Clive's victory over the Nawab of Bengal and his French backers at Plassey in 1757, which resulted in British dominance in India, and James Wolfe's victory on the Plains of Abraham in 1759, which brought Canada under the Crown, were two severe blows to France – Britain's major European rival on foreign shores. By 1788, the first British settlement was established in Australia; in 1806 the British took control of the Cape of Good Hope in South Africa and in 1840 the British settlement at Wellington in New Zealand began.

Britain's growing empire, like all empires, was in part an empire by conquest and in part an empire by economic control. Famously, the arteries of the Roman and Inca empires were their extensive road systems. For the British Empire, its lifeblood was carried by sea. Although it extended over vast lands, it was essentially a maritime empire, forged and maintained by military and merchant fleets, the scale of which the world had not seen before.

The British Navy was the envy of the world. For 350 years, from the defeat of the Spanish Armada in 1588, the Royal Navy was the envy of the world. It allowed Britain to impose its will on its empire, as well as to thwart any foreign challenge to its possessions. The British merchant fleet held similar sway over international trade, facilitating an exchange of goods that granted the Empire its economic imperative.

Ironically, almost at the point that the Empire developed its greatest momentum, it suffered its greatest reversal. However, the Declaration of Independence by the American colonies in 1776, and its acceptance by Britain in 1782, although a severe blow, hardly affected imperial growth. In some ways,

it shifted the emphasis away from squabbles over government with white, former-British cousins, to wars of conquest with non-white foreigners in far-away lands. Africa and Asia were "virgin" territories and were far easier to subdue and govern.

However, before Britannia could rule the world at the beginning of the nineteenth century, the not insignificant matter of France – resurgent, revolutionary and guided by a charismatic figure capable of creating an empire entirely through his own ambition – had to be dealt with. For a while, Napoleon, his *Grande Armée* and his European power-base threatened not only Britain's pre-eminence, but Britain itself. It was indeed "a close-run thing", but in Admiral Nelson – notably at the Battle of Trafalgar (1805) – and the Duke of Wellington – in the Peninsular War in Spain (1808–14) and at the Battle of Waterloo (1815) – Britain found military leaders who could contain Napoleon's flamboyant aggression.

Victory over Napoleonic France brought more territory for Britain and an even greater sense of righteous invincibility. Revolutionary ideology was defeated (thus consigning to history the bad memories of the loss of the American colonies) and a dangerous demagogue tamed. Britain's moral superiority was confirmed – at least to its own citizen's satisfaction. Its merchants, sailors, soldiers and adventurers could go forth unhindered and civilize the world.

RULER OF THE WAVES

In its earliest days, the British Empire was a maritime empire, based on the strength of the Royal Navy and the trade of its merchant fleet. The world's great ports and harbours were the vital footholds of Britain's economic and strategic power. Gibraltar, Malta, Aden, Bombay, Penang, Singapore, Sydney, Cape Town and many others were essential to the future growth of the Empire.

Below The 1588 victory over the fleet of Philip II, the King of Spain, was testament to the growing strength of the English navy (seen on the left). It confirmed Sir Francis Drake as the leading seaman of his era and consolidated the power of the reign of Elizabeth I of England. Painted by John Pine (1660–1756).

Right Henry VII (1457–1509), the patron of John Cabot's (Genoese explorer, Giovanni Caboto) voyage to the east coast of North America in 1497. A painting by Francesco Grisellini, 1761.

WORLD TRADE

Trade was the lifeblood of the British Empire. Trading companies like the East India Company (founded in India in 1600) and the Hudson's Bay Company (granted the charter to trade, principally in furs, in Canada in 1670) provided the entrepreneurial skills and dynamism to make the business of empire flourish.

Right Native troops in the East India Company's service: a trooper of the bodyguard of the Governor General, a private of the Bengal Regular Cavalry and a private of the Java Volunteers. An engraving by Joseph Constantine Stadler, 1815.

AMERICAN INDEPENDENCE

It is ironic that long before the Empire reached its zenith, Britain "lost" the territory which had the greatest military and economic potential and which would – much later – become a world superpower. The defection of the American colonies in 1776 was a severe blow, but trade links were quickly re-established and British strategic dominance of the Atlantic from Canada to the West Indies remained intact.

Below The Declaration of Independence by the founding 13 states of the United States of America, July 4, 1776.

THE FRENCH THREAT

Britain had many European rivals for world supremacy, not least of which was France. A resurgent French republic, under its charismatic leader Napoleon Bonaparte, became a real threat, not only to Britain's pre-eminent position in the world, but also to Britain itself. British military victories in Egypt, Spain and, finally, at Waterloo in 1815, led by its famous heroes, Lord Nelson and the Duke of Wellington, brought about a long period of relative stability in Europe and British dominance throughout the world.

Above The Battle of Trafalgar, 21 October 1805.
Admiral Nelson's famous victory. A painting by
William Clarkson-Stanfield (1793–1867).

Opposite The Battle of Waterloo, 18 June
1815. Victory for Britain and its allies, led by
the Duke of Wellington. A painting by Denis
Dighton (1792–1827).

Right "The Army and the Navy". A painting of the Duke of
Wellington and Admiral Lord Nelson by John Prescott
Knight (1803–1881).

NEW COLONIES

Britain's military prowess during the latter part of the eighteenth century made
it possible for British adventurers and settlers to claim and colonize more and
more territory. This was particularly true in lands previously not permanently
occupied by Europeans, in Africa, the Far East and Australasia.

Above A naval engagement between the French and British off the Cape of Good Hope, South Africa,
March 9, 1757. The period between 1755 and 1763 was a time of attritional naval battles between
Britain and France across the oceans of the world. Victory by the Royal Navy led France to relinquish its
claims to Canada in the Treaty of Paris (1763) and confirmed the power of the British Empire. A
painting by Samuel Scott (1702–72)

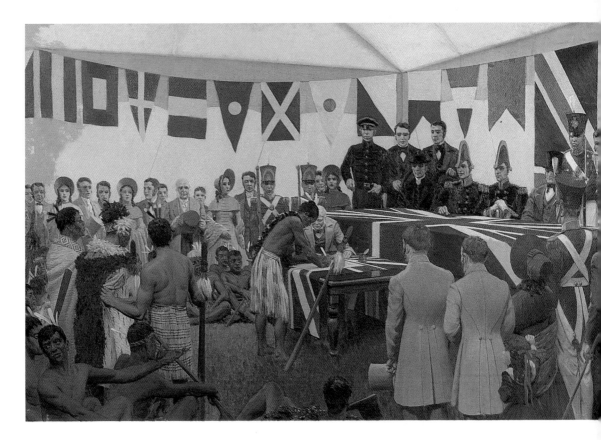

Right The signing of the Treaty of Waitangi by Captain William Hobson and large numbers of Maori chiefs in 1840. The treaty marked the formal assumption of British sovereignty over New Zealand, but led to many years of turmoil and resistance to European settlers. A painting by Marcus King.

Left
"The Emigrants". Throughout the nineteenth century, thousands of British families, like this idealized Scottish family of ten surrounded by their worldly goods, left Britain to settle in the new territories of the Empire. A painting by W. Allsworth *circa* 1850.

1815–1918
PAX BRITANNICA?

The nineteenth century was Britain's century. Full of pride, the British bestrode their empire of 11 million square miles; its 400 million subjects turned to London in wonder and awe; its Union Jack and red-coated soldiers became icons of security and stability. Some authors have even likened the era to the Roman Peace of the first-century emperors of Rome and christened it the *Pax Britannica*. Britain's industrial revolution sucked people into its sprawling cities and spewed out goods across the world. The rural poor, dispossessed by agricultural revolution, provided a steady stream of eager emigrants to populate seemingly empty countries such as Australia and New Zealand.

The Empire took many forms. There was direct rule and occupation, but, by contrast, many areas were governed by treaties with local potentates and princes who would be reminded of their responsibilities by a visit from the Royal Navy in the policy that became known as "gunboat diplomacy". There was also an "informal" empire. British military influence and economic power meant that many parts of the world that were not formally a part of the Empire fell within the British sphere of influence. This was particularly true in South America and for what was called Britain's "practical protectorate" over the Turkish Empire.

But, like the Roman Peace, the *Pax Britannica* was not consensual. Rule, either paternal or repressive, was enforced. Broadly speaking, British imperialists fell into two philosophical positions: the authoritarians, often those, like servicemen and district administrators, who had to deal with the workings of empire at the sharp end, and who felt that their colonial subjects were inferior and should be treated accordingly, and the idealists, often missionaries and educationalists, who felt that the Empire could provide a model of culture and enlightenment for native peoples to aspire to and better themselves by. The two schools of thought fought out their differences over the issue of slavery.

To its credit, Britain abolished the slave trade in 1807, and in 1808, Sierra Leone in West Africa became a Crown Colony and a model of paternalism as it strove to "introduce civilization among the natives". Squadrons of British warships were despatched, to arrest slavers not only off the West African coast, but also in the Indian and Pacific Oceans. However, it proved to be more difficult to abolish the institution of slave labour in the Empire.

Resistance from the Caribbean plantations in particular meant that it wasn't abolished until 1833. Ironically, abolition led to a shortage of plantation workers, resulting in the reinstitution of the practice of indenturing servants – many of them poor Chinese and Indians – who were despatched to all corners of the Empire as cheap labour.

Perhaps the most powerful of all carriers of the imperial message were God's soldiers, the missionaries. They took the "muscular Christianity" of Victorian Britain and imposed it on the world. These were the men who gave the world English games, English fair play and the caricatured stiff upper lip of good Christian Englishmen "standing firm in the face of savagery and adversity".

However, when the paternalism of the British idealists was rejected, as in the Indian Rebellion of 1857, then the iron fist of the British authoritarians prevailed. The mutiny was crushed with a terrible ferocity and the hostility of British people towards the "coloured" races of the Empire rose in waves, as lurid stories of atrocities committed against defenceless British women and children filled the columns of British newspapers.

Equally depressing for the idealists of the Empire were the Maori wars in New Zealand. As in South Africa, Australia and Canada, hopes that British emigrants and native peoples could live happily side-by-side were shattered. For over 30 years, from 1840 onwards, the Maoris fought to regain their land and control over their culture before eventually being subdued by the colonists. Regardless of the intention, throughout the nineteenth century these four territories – the Canadian provinces, the Australian states, New Zealand and the Cape Colony – became the "white" Empire. Each was granted a large degree of self-government and each became a haven for the disaffected, the ambitious and the adventurous. In time, these self-governing colonies matured into large, politically stable territories. The Canadian colonies embarked upon confederation in 1867. Federation followed for the Australian colonies in 1901 and, after the trauma of the Boer War, for the South African colonies in 1910. As the direct political ties with Britain were loosened, so the colonies' local characteristics came to the fore, characteristics that would later come to typify them as nations.

With the notable exception of India, where British rulers occupied lands previously governed by Hindu princes and Mughal emperors, the greater part of the Empire had to be carved from lands regarded as "virgin" territory. Men like Frederick Lugard in East Africa, Cecil Rhodes in southern Africa and Stamford Raffles in the Far East, used their tenacity and harnessed their personal ambitions and dreams to carve out new territory for the Empire.

The "scramble for Africa" was typical. It became the "white man's burden", as Kipling called it, to lead Africa out of its supposedly savage ways along the path towards civilization. In 1870, the greater part of the interior of the African continent was, to European eyes, unexplored and unclaimed. But by the turn of the twentieth century, Britain had grabbed for itself large chunks of eastern and southern Africa and, in a bizarre mix of rivalry and gentleman's agreement with the French, had also acquired the whole of West Africa from the Sahara Desert to the Congo River.

In 1897, Queen Victoria celebrated her Diamond Jubilee – an event which with hindsight stands out as the zenith of the British Empire. The twentieth century beckoned – a century of new technology and innovation; a century of wealth and opportunity.

Britain was primed and ready to exploit it and control it. This was a new Rome. *The Times* reported the procession to St Paul's to mark the Jubilee as a "wonderful exhibition of allegiance and brotherhood amongst so many myriads of men... The mightiest and most beneficial Empire ever known in the annals of mankind."

The long and bloody war against the Boers, the descendants of the Dutch settlers of South Africa, which started in 1899, did not quell the jingoistic rhetoric of the time. Although it was a real crisis, involving the commitment of over 200,000 imperial troops (including thousands of New Zealanders, Australians and Canadians), the Boer revolt was crushed, and within a few years Britain had developed a successful accommodation with the Boers (the Afrikaners) and their leader, Jan Smuts, which would survive for half a century. The Boer War was not the turning point for the Empire. It was to be another war, 15 years later, that would reveal the inherent fragility of an empire which seemed so mighty. The modern world, which heralded so much for Britain's hegemony, would, in fact, be its undoing.

But at the beginning of the twentieth century, for most Britons, and for many colonial subjects, the Empire still inspired hope and pride and promised new opportunities. How could the future be a threat to the Empire, when the Empire itself was forging the future? During this period, tens of thousands of people left Britain's shores to find new lives in the colonies.

Over 20 million people left the British Isles between 1815 and 1914. Irish peasants fled the agony of famine; miners and agricultural labourers escaped the hardships and poverty of Wales, Cornwall and northern England and disgruntled Scots preferred the prospect of opportunity in distant lands to the misery of life at home. Sprinkled among the vast majority of "have-nots" were missionaries, teachers, engineers, planters, and entrepreneurs, who varied in ethical complexion from idealists to carpetbaggers. Ironically, most washed up not in the Empire, but in the United States. However, the greater part of the remainder arrived in Canada, Australia, New Zealand and South Africa.

For many expatriate British, life was more stereotypically "British" in the colonies than in Britain. British conventions, habits and pastimes were rigidly adhered to. Cricket, football and tennis were pursued avidly. Riding, hunting and shooting were *de rigueur*. Drinking was not only thought to be an appropriate social custom, but was also thought to provide a barrier against tropical diseases, the rigours of a hot climate and general foreign malaise. "The Club" became the hub of colonial life; sumptuous or modest, it was a little corner of home. The local travellers' hotel or bar, with English beer and furniture, looked, sounded and smelled like the old country.

For many in the colonies, the perks of life were plentiful and cheap: tea on the lawn, champagne before dinner, horses and hounds; safaris and sightseeing, sailing and climbing, entertaining and entertainment; all were available, to those of modest means.

Perhaps the single most alluring feature of colonial life was adventure. The physical challenges involved in discovering, mining and farming "virgin" land were immense. The complexities and dangers of building new railways, bridges and dams were considerable, while the day-to-day dilemmas and anxieties of policing, educating and administering native peoples were daunting. For young Edwardians, spurred by the derring-do of their Victorian fathers and grandfathers, it was as if they were enacting a role in an adventure novel. Mountains, rivers, savannahs, deserts and frozen waters were there to be subdued. Armed only with their inherent Britishness, out they stepped to meet the test. Little was written about the unbearable reality of disease, fatigue, hunger, cold and heat, for such stories would have spoiled the adventure.

While Britain seemed content ruling its empire, its neighbours in Europe had moved on: Tsarist Russia was now expansionist and ambitious; France had rediscovered the military *élan* of past glories; and the newly unified nations of Germany and Italy were hungry for conquests to fulfil what they perceived to be ancient destinies. The previous European balance of power, so vital to the *Pax Britannica*, was about to collapse. Moreover, one of Britain's original colonies, the young and brash United States of America, was about to assert itself. The twentieth century would not be Britain's domain, nor even a European one: it would be American.

Although the Great War was a watershed for the British Empire, revealing its inherent contradictions and illustrating the changing rules of global politics that would eventually lead to its downfall, it was, in many ways, also the Empire's finest hour.

In the "Great War for Civilization", as the First World War came to be called, all Britain's vainglorious claims for the purpose and value of its empire appeared to be substantiated. Its various peoples fought for a common cause. Over 60,000 Indians, nearly 60,000 Australians, 56,000 Canadians and almost 17,000 New Zealanders died. Africans, West Indians, Chinese, Maoris and Egyptians served with distinction. South Africa contributed over 130,000 white troops, 7,000 of whom died, and over 40,000 black labourers and auxiliary forces.

When the war was over, Lord Curzon summed up the prevailing mood of self-satisfaction: "The British flag never flew over more powerful or united an empire than now; never did our voice count for more in the councils of the nations, or in determining the future destinies of mankind." As with the defeat of Napoleon a hundred years earlier, and the numerous victories on colonial battlegrounds around the world – Omdurman, Rorke's Drift, Mafeking – Britain's innate superiority seemed to have been proven yet again. But, on the contrary, the myth of British superiority had been exploded.

It was, in fact, the crucial intervention of the United States, towards the end of the war in 1917, which had tipped the military scales against Germany. But, even more significantly, the psychology of the Empire had changed. Not only had the sheer brutality and horror of the conflict led men to question what had been almost instinctive loyalties, but an empire superficially united in arms on the battlefield had found that huge schisms of class, race and culture ran under the surface. Australians, from a fluid social background of "mateship" and camaraderie, found the rigid distinctions of rank in the British army unacceptable, the arrogance of the British officer detestable and the subservience of the British soldier contemptible. For Australians, for New Zealanders and for Canadians the experience of war did not reinforce how close they were to Britain, but how far away they were.

For men from the non-white regions of the Empire, service in the cause of the king was no less disconcerting. Encouraged to enlist, they immediately found that they were not just seen as second-class soldiers, but, in many cases, were considered not good enough to be regarded as soldiers at all. They were employed as labourers, cooks, cleaners and orderlies. The hierarchy of the British army was happy to have their labour, but nervous that if given an opportunity to kill white Germans they might get a taste for shooting at white soldiers upon their return to their homes. Similarly, many British officers, who had few doubts that black servicemen could fight, recoiled in horror at the prospect of their wounded being cared for by British nurses.

For Indians, Africans and West Indians, service for the Crown represented, both literally and metaphorically, a significant broadening of their horizons. Despite being treated as inferiors, they returned to their countries better informed, more experienced and more able to understand the British. They had seen not just the aloof and arrogant officers of the British elite, but also the ordinary British soldier and civilian, many of whom also appeared to be treated as inferior and who were often less sophisticated or less educated than they were. Many returned to their countries conscious for the first time of the potential they and their people might have.

The Empire took pride in its triumph. On the surface, it grew stronger and it certainly acquired more territory as a consequence of the peace settlement at the end of the war. But, in reality the death and suffering of the First World War and the new world order it beckoned marked the end of the glories of the *Pax Britannica*.

THE EMPIRE BUILDERS

There were many explorers, adventurers and opportunists who contributed to the growth of the British Empire. Their intrepidness was often borne of either naïve idealism or ruthless ambition; or of all shades of motivation in between. Countless numbers of soldiers, administrators, missionaries, engineers and teachers became the pillars of the Empire.

Right "Cecil Rhodes" by Howard Davie. Rhodes, a vicar's son born in Bishop's Stortford, made a fortune in the Kimberley diamond mines before becoming the most dominant force in the politics of Southern Africa from 1890 until his death in 1902.

Left Stamford Raffles (1781–1826) was one of the major founders of Britain's empire in East Asia. Following postings in Malacca, Java and Sumatra, he secured the transfer of Singapore to the East India Company in 1819 and initiated policies that contributed greatly to Singapore's vital role in the lucrative China trade. Raffles was reknowned for his liberal attitude toward peoples under colonial rule, his rigorous suppression of the slave trade, and his enthusiasm for collecting historical and scientific information.

Above The Canadian Hall at the Great Exhibition in 1851. From *Dickinson's Comprehensive Pictures*. The exhibition was designed to celebrate the "Works of Industry of all Nations", but was, in reality, a symbolic statement of Britain's wealth and power.

Above "The Charge of the Queen's Bays against Mutineers at Lucknow, India, March 1859". By Henry Payne (1868–1940). There were many colourful representations of derring-do and brave deeds by British soldiers in defence of the Empire, designed to reinforce patriotic feelings about Britain's imperial policy.

Left "Uniforms of the Colonial Armies" by P.H. Michel, an illustration from *Le Petit Journal*, circa 1883. Just a few of the many British and colonial troops enlisted to guard the Empire against enemies from without and within.

EMPRESS OF INDIA

Queen Victoria was the great maternal figure of the Empire. She was queen from 1837 until her death in 1901 and was proclaimed Empress of India in 1876. Her Golden Jubilee in 1887 and, in particular, her Diamond Jubilee in 1897 were highpoints of British pride in its Empire. Victoria's long reign came to be associated with the golden age of British imperial power.

Right "The Diamond Jubilee of Queen Victoria" by G.S. Amato, 1897. The most splendidly colourful occasion London had ever witnessed. Loyal subjects had travelled from every corner of the Empire to pay tribute to their queen and empress.

Left "The Delhi Durbar", an illustration from *Le Petit Journal*, January 1903. Durbars were held at regular intervals to mark special imperial occasions like coronations and jubilees. They were vast military parades of pomp and splendour.

THE BOER WAR

At the height of Britain's imperial power, it became embroiled in a major conflict in South Africa. Between 1899 and 1902, British forces fought a fierce war against the Boers of South Africa. The Boers were settlers of Dutch descent, bitterly opposed to British rule. British garrisons at Ladysmith and Mafeking were besieged and then relieved in famous incidents, and a vicious guerrilla war was fought out across the country's vast hinterland. Britain used "concentration" camps to incarcerate Boer women and children in order to persuade the Boer guerrilla leaders to capitulate.

Left "The Death of the Boer General Viljoen in the Transvaal" by Eugene Damblans. The front cover of *Le Petit Journal*, 5 November, 1899.

Left "Peace with the Boers", an illustration from *Le Petit Journal*, 1902. Peace came as a great relief to a British public not used to such an audacious challenge to British dominance. More than 5,000 British soldiers died during the conflict. Boer losses were greater than 4,000. In addition, it has been estimated that over 20,000 Boer women and children died of disease and neglect in British concentration camps.

Below South African leader Jan Smuts at home in his garden in South Africa (1946). Smuts was born in the Cape Colony in 1870 and educated at Cambridge. He fought in the Boer War with General Jacobus de la Rey and was prime minister of the Union of South Africa from 1919–24 and 1939–48. Essentially pro-British, he was defeated by the Nationalist Party in 1948.

DAWN OF A NEW CENTURY

The twentieth century arrived with Britain proudly surveying its vast empire around the world. But the new century would be a century of such rapid change and development that Britain's Empire would soon be overwhelmed. What had been over five hundred years in the making would be all but gone in little more than fifty tumultuous years.

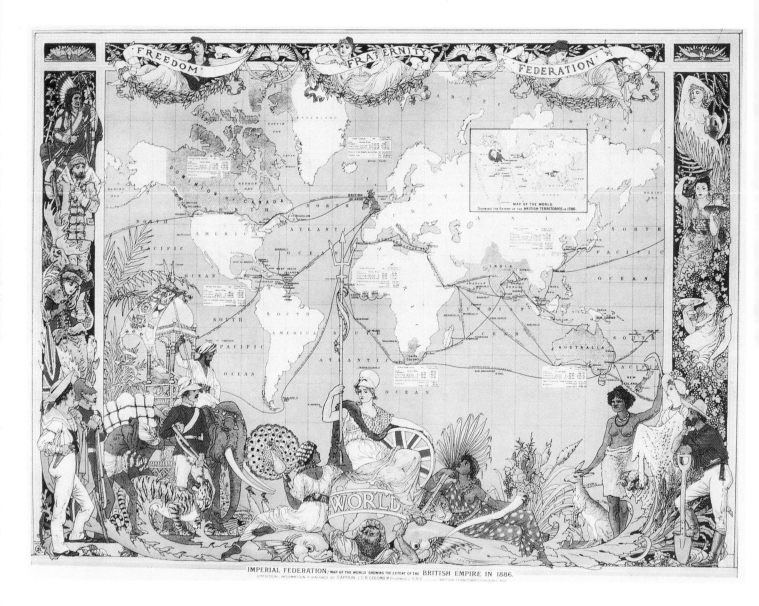

Above "Freedom, Fraternity, Liberation" by Captain J.C. Columbo, 1886. Britannia sits regally on her world, while her admiring subjects gaze at the map of her many conquests.

Above "The Coronation of Edward VII", 1902. The new king welcomes Indian maharajahs to his coronation in London. Although well over sixty by the time he ascended the throne, and with a tarnished reputation for being less than discreet in his private life, his Edwardian Age became a period of relative contentment and affluence as Britain basked in the glory of its Empire.

Right "Red Indians at Buckingham Palace". From *Le Petit Journal*, September 1906. Like a scene from imperial Rome, or Egypt of the pharaohs, the Empire's many subjects place tributes at the feet of the king and emperor, Edward VII, and his queen, Alexandra.

THE FIRST WORLD WAR

Britain's Edwardian era would be a short-lived interlude of peace and prosperity. Edward VII died in 1910. There would be no second, glorious "Georgian Britain" under the new king, George V. The horror of world war saw to that. Political rivalries in Europe, especially the rise of a powerful and expansionist Germany, upset the balance of power and created a catastrophic war that has been called both the "end of innocence" and "the beginning of the end of the British Empire".

Above "Let's Go Canada", a recruitment poster for Canadian soldiers, 1914. Canadians, like all their comrades in the Empire, rushed to fight for the cause.

Left "Coo-ee", a recruitment poster for South Australia, 1914. The British Empire would fight as one during the First World War.

Above Australian 2nd Division Pioneers, clearing a road in Ypres, Belgium, October 1917. The fighting on the Ypres Salient was among the bloodiest of the entire war.

Left British tanks, stuck in the interminable mud of the Western Front, near Ypres, Belgium, 1917.

Above Pilots from No. 1 Squadron, Australia
Flying Corps, Medjel Aerodrome, 1918.

Opposite British Empire troops fought a long
campaign in the Middle East during the First
World War. This overturned steam-driven
transporter is on the supply route between
Jerusalem and Jericho, Palestine, 1918.

Left Another view of the supply route for guns and provisions along the road from Jerusalem to Jericho. The Jordan Valley is in the background, Palestine, 1918.

Below A group of men camped in the desert, a detachment of the Australian Light Horse Regiment, Belah, Palestine, February 1918. The Australian Light Horse Regiment, together with the New Zealand Mounted Rifles and several Indian cavalry units, played a major part in the campaign in Palestine against Turkey.

Above In a scene more reminiscent of the Western Front, troops negotiating a flooded *wadi* near Ludd, Palestine, Christmas 1917.

Right An impressive formation of the 4th Australian Light Horse Regiment, Gaza, Palestine, January 1918. Gaza had only recently been abandoned by its Turkish defenders on 6 November 1917.

1919–1945
LENGTHENING SHADOWS

Although the traumatic experiences of the First World War, and the strategic and political changes it heralded, were a significant turning point in the history of the British Empire, this was not apparent at the time. For most people, both the rulers and the ruled, the traumas and irregularities of life created by the war needed to be put behind them as soon as possible. Stability and security were important comforts. A dangerous enemy – made almost bestial by powerful propaganda – had been defeated. Now, life could return to normal.

After all, the Empire had fought and won as one. The Royal Navy had contained the German fleet and had proved itself, once again, to be the most powerful weapon in the world. Besides, there were new territories to mould and Anglicize. They would need the velvet glove of British paternalism and, if needs be, the mailed fist of British authority. Old habits die hard.

In the peace settlement following the First World War, nearly a million square miles were added to the Empire, along with 13 million new subjects. Many of the new territories brought a psychological "completeness" to some of Britain's proudest colonial ambitions. German South West Africa completed the British hegemony of southern Africa. The acquisition of Tanganyika (German East Africa) finally realized the dream of Cecil Rhodes, that Britain would rule in Africa from Cairo to the Cape. In the Middle East, Iraq, Transjordan and Palestine became British mandates, while Persia became, to all intents and purposes, a British protectorate. Thus, if one so desired, and had the means, it was possible to journey from Cape Town to Rangoon under the protection of the British sphere of influence. From the frozen waters of northern Canada to the snow-capped peaks of New Zealand's Southern Alps; from the jungles of British Guiana in South America, across the Earth's widest girth, to the remote Pitcairn Island in the southern Pacific, the world really was coloured red. Every British child knew what was literally true – that the sun never set on the British Empire.

But even in the granting of these new territories, there was set ticking a timing mechanism of expectation that would irrevocably undermine the Empire, not strengthen it. The Versailles Treaty and the peace settlements at the end of the First World War, which ceded these territories to Britain, were not intended to be an imperial carve-up. The "Fourteen Points" of the United States president, Woodrow Wilson, and the League of Nations, which followed in 1919, specified a new basis for the affairs of the world. There was to be a "sacred trust" between those mandated to protect the territories and the "subject peoples" of those territories. The covenant of the League of Nations was clear. In the mandated areas, the interests of both governors and governed were to be considered equal. That this new ethical framework should emanate from a president of the United States was both prophetic and ironic: prophetic in that it would be the United States which would soon replace Britain at the forefront of world affairs; and ironic in that it was the people of the American colonies who had first asserted their rights within the Empire some 150 years earlier. It was as if the Empire had been living on borrowed time ever since. Indeed, it would go on doing so for a while yet, despite the cracks which soon appeared.

In 1916, there had been a major armed rebellion against British rule in Ireland (the Easter Rising) and in 1919 *Sinn Féin*, the Irish Republican movement, proclaimed Ireland a republic. Although the revolt was crushed, the momentum for independence was now irresistible. After a savage civil war, Britain finally agreed in 1921 to the creation of the Irish Free State, a self-governing dominion that would have equal status and rights to those of Canada. In 1922 the country was partitioned, and the six heavily Protestant counties of the north-east, having previously elected to remain under British rule, were joined together as Northern Ireland.

Despite the first major crack in the grand edifice of "Britishness" that was implicit in Irish independence, the Empire soldiered on. There were problems with Turkey to be dealt with and the demands of possessions spanning the entire globe grew and grew. Both morale and propaganda for the task were provided by the British Empire Exhibition in 1924.

With a new cathedral of sport as its centrepiece, London's Wembley was transformed into a "World's Fair", a homage to Britain's rule in many lands. The force of authority certainly seemed to be with the British. Rudyard Kipling himself named the streets of the exhibition, Edward Elgar conducted the massed choirs at the opening ceremony and the architectural designs of Edwin Lutyens lent imperial solemnity to the events. It was hugely popular, perhaps more as a funfair than as a symbol of national pride, but was yet another reminder that the hard-won possessions of 250 years of history would not be easily rescinded.

The Middle East was proving to be just as intractable as Ireland had been. Unease and revolt in many Arab states, particularly Iraq, was expensive to contain. The British army had fought the most devastating war in history and needed frequent replenishment. The British taxpayer was increasingly reluctant to fund foreign adventure, especially when, in the early 1920s, unemployment in Britain started to rise. Ultimately, British pragmatism prevailed and treaties were signed in Iraq, Egypt and Transjordan with leaders who would be strong enough to rule their territories, but loyal enough to Britain to allow *de facto* British control to continue. This would prove to be of particular strategic importance in the region over the next few years, as oil, the "black gold" of the area, became an increasingly important commodity for the world economy.

In Palestine, British attempts to maintain order were undermined by developments outside the Middle East. British foreign secretary Arthur Balfour had, in 1917, declared the British government's sympathy with the idea of a national home in Palestine for the Jewish people. By the 1930s, there were increasing numbers of Jewish settlers in Palestine, driven there partly by optimism for a state of their own but mainly to escape growing anti-Semitism in Europe, particularly in Adolf Hitler's Germany. As the 1930s wore on, and a major war became a frightening possibility, Britain felt it had little choice but to pacify Arab interests in order to protect her oil supplies. In 1939, Britain announced that Jewish immigration would be limited to 25,000 a year and that plans would be drawn up for an independent state with a permanent Arab majority. This produced a period of relative calm, but it would only be temporary. Events unfolding elsewhere would soon change forever the dynamics of the politics in the Holy Land.

No matter what trials and tribulations faced Britain and its Empire as the twentieth century became increasingly tumultuous, the greatest prize still shone: India, the jewel in the crown of imperial glory. The Raj (a word originally from ancient Sanskrit, borrowed by the British from Hindi, meaning "kingdom") gave the Empire its symbolic heart and allowed the ancient kings and queens of the British Isles to adopt the ultimate accolade of emperor or empress. India had become as much myth as reality. A vast area of countless numbers of people, home to ancient cultures and kingdoms, a land of huge wealth alongside unimaginable poverty, India enchanted the British. Detractors claim that the British exploited India, abusing and patronizing its people, and stealing its wealth; apologists claim that Britain created the dream of a vast, diverse nation from ancient chaos and oppression. Wherever the truth lies between these views, India offered a remarkable experience for all who lived there and for all who visited it in its imperial prime. But it also witnessed tragedies.

India in 1919 was a troubled land. Riots and demonstrations swept the country. Amritsar in the Punjab, home to the Golden Temple, the most sacred site of the Sikh religion, was particularly tense. Five Englishmen had been killed and a female English missionary had been assaulted. All demonstrations were banned and when a large crowd gathered in the Jallianwalla Bagh (a large sunken garden, surrounded by high walls) a senior British officer initiated an act of astonishing brutality.

Brigadier-General Reginald Dyer deployed a small detachment of Gurkha and Baluchi troops on high ground, who then, without warning, opened fire. There was carnage in the tightly-packed crowd, as the volleys of fire continued for over six minutes. There were few escape routes; those that were available became particular targets for the British colonial soldiers and soon became blocked by piles of bodies. The official death toll was 379. Dyer's only expression of regret about the incident was that he had been unable to use the machine guns he had had mounted on his armoured cars.

The massacre was a turning point in Indian history. It confirmed the view, propagated by the Indian nationalist leadership, that British rule was little more than a brutal foreign regime. It also exacerbated divisions in Britain about the morality of imperial rule. The debate about Dyer's actions was vehement. Although he was officially castigated for the massacre, right-wing diehards defended him vociferously. *The Morning Post* opened a fund for him, which raised £26,000, including a donation from Rudyard Kipling.

While Britain wrestled with the ethics of its behaviour towards the Indians, India found a leader whose remarkable character would leave an indelible mark on the modern world: Mahatma Gandhi, the "Pure Soul"; a man many thought a saint; a man who many others regarded as an interfering trouble-maker. The British tried imprisoning him, but the quality of his spiritual leadership was such that he became the beacon of hope for the entire subcontinent.

In 1931, Gandhi organized a revolt of blinding simplicity: a systematic programme of producing and selling salt, which was supposed to be a government monopoly. A wave of illicit salt collecting, led by the Mahatma himself, swept India. The British felt they had no choice but to arrest Gandhi, along with most of the leadership of India's biggest nationalist party, the Indian National Congress. But Gandhi's simple cry for freedom, his complex and mystifying philosophy and his powerful campaigns of civil disobedience were winning friends around the world. Britain had to make a series of tactical withdrawals. First, he was released, then he parleyed with the viceroy and, finally, he went to London, where he charmed many ordinary Britons and took tea with the king (who was, of course, also Gandhi's emperor). But, by 1935, independence for India seemed inevitable, no matter how those for whom the Empire was an imperative of life – like Winston Churchill – strove to prevent it.

1935 was also the year of the Silver Jubilee of King George V and, once again, Britain had a chance to parade itself, to show the world how mighty it was, and to demonstrate how its Empire remained as strong as ever. The pageantry of the Jubilee included the brightly coloured tunics, plumes, braid and tassels of troops from all over the world. London reverberated with the strident music of scores of military bands, the clattering of feet and hooves of seemingly countless infantry and cavalry and the incessant cheering of an intoxicated crowd. For older witnesses, who could remember Victoria's Diamond Jubilee in 1897, it must have been as if nothing had changed. But a great deal had changed. Never again would such splendour be seen on the streets of London. The First World War had brought the *Pax Britannica* to an end. The second great war of the twentieth century, one that was about to engulf the world, would mark the beginning of the end for the Empire. However, before its inevitable demise became a reality, it would – as it had in the First World War – acquit itself magnificently.

The German dictator, Adolf Hitler, had come to power in 1933. His ambitions were hardly obscure. His virulent speeches, his polemical writing and his overtly aggressive demeanour all made clear his burning ambition: to establish a new and all-powerful Germany. Although the British Prime Minister, Neville Chamberlain, and his French allies tried appeasing Hitler's desire for conquest, the Second World War unleashed its terror on the world in September 1939. Following the fall of France in June 1940, Britain stood isolated and alone in the face of Hitler's onslaught. The United States and the Soviet Union, the two superpowers of the future, became the great wells of strength upon which the Allies could draw, but it was Britain and her Empire which faced the brunt of the initial fighting – not only against Germany in Europe, but also against Japan and in Asia when the Japanese entered the war in 1941.

To a much greater extent than during the First World War, Britain's ability to play a central role in a global conflict depended on the support of the Empire, particularly the white dominions. Britain's war strategy was outlined to the dominion governments as early as 1937, at a Commonwealth Conference in London, the first for six years. A crucial part of British tactics at the Conference was to suggest to the dominions that they needed Britain as much as Britain needed the dominions. The Australians and New Zealanders, in particular, were not convinced. They were especially anxious that the British, concentrating on defending Britain in Europe, might have neither the resources nor the will to defend the Empire's interests in South East Asia – particularly the strategically vital city of Singapore. As Japan began to move southwards at the beginning of the war, it became increasingly apparent that Britain would be unable to mount a serious naval (and certainly land-based) defence of its interests in the Far East. Australia and New Zealand had little choice but to look to the United States for a more likely source of help. Not since the American War of Independence, 160 years earlier, had Britain been unable to defend itself on a global scale.

Despite these obvious difficulties, the emotional and strategic bonds of Empire were still strong. When war was declared, the Empire did its duty, but now with a cool and calculating rationale, rather than the naïve euphoria of 1914: Britain needed the Empire and the Empire needed Britain, at least for the time being. Robert Menzies, the Australian Prime Minister, put it succinctly: "We in Australia are involved because the destruction or defeat of Great Britain would be the destruction of the British Empire, and leave us with precarious tenure of our own independence."

Although the Empire was still intact and although it remained true that the sun never set on the British Empire, it was late in the day. Soon the shadows that would herald the going down of the sun would cast their rapidly lengthening gloom over more than 200 years of imperial history.

INDIA: JEWEL IN THE CROWN

India became the most lauded possession of the British Empire. The Raj became the "jewel in the crown" of British Imperial rule when resistance to the British presence was overcome after the Indian Rebellion of 1857. At that point, power was transferred from the East India Company – which had effectively consolidated British control of the subcontinent, especially against rival French claims, during the preceding 250 years – to the British government in London.

Above The Taj Mahal, photographed sometime between 1910 and 1920. The Taj Mahal was built by the Mughal emperor Shah Jahan as a mausoleum in memory of his wife, Arjumand Banu Begam, who died in childbirth in 1631. The whole project was completed around 1650.

Right A Guard of Honour, Bombay, India, 1921. The Indian Army was regarded as an asset of great strategic importance. It was not only vital to British rule in India, it was also deployed to great effect in Europe, the Middle East and Far East during both world wars.

Left The garden of a grand house in Bombay, *circa* 1910–1920. For the British elite in India, life in the Raj could be very luxurious. Large houses with numerous servants allowed them to more than match the lifestyle of their social equivalents at home in Britain.

Left A group of men outside a temple, *circa* 1925. India is a country of diverse ethnic, cultural and religious traditions. Hinduism is the major religion, but there are also significant communities of Muslims, Christians, Sikhs, Jains and Buddhists.

Right Group of Indian men outside a temple *circa* 1910.

Above A guard standing in a courtyard, India *circa* 1910.

Above The entrance to one of Calcutta's spectacular temples, possibly the Jain Temple, situated on the banks of the Hugli, photographed *circa* 1920.

Right A posed portrait of an Indian man standing on a decorative bridge in formal gardens, *circa* 1920.

Left A "Mr Geogardi", posing amid the floral beauty of an Indian garden in Calcutta around the time of the First World War.

Above The Savoy Hotel, *circa* 1920. Three men enjoy the comfort of the hotel garden.

Opposite A bride posing in her costume, Darjeeling, *circa* 1910. It is probable from her appearance, that this is a British woman displaying a traditional bridal outfit.

CEYLON

Ceylon, now known as Sri Lanka, became a crown colony of the British Empire in 1802, when the British captured the former Dutch colony. Tea production was a vital industry during British rule and remained so after independence in 1948.

Above Two girls pose for the camera in Kandy, Ceylon, around the turn of the twentieth century. Three-quarters of the population were ethnic Sinhalese, followed by a significant number of Tamils.

Below "Dr Parsons and Dr G", Queen's House,
Colombo, Ceylon. Photographed, "on the occasion of
the king's birthday", probably in the 1920s.

EGYPT

The ancient land of Egypt came under British control in 1882, allowing Britain to protect the vitally important sea route, the Suez Canal (completed in 1867). The British army remained in Egypt, despite Egypt being granted limited sovereignty under King Faud (1922) and later King Farouk (1936–52). British influence ended in 1953 when King Farouk fled the country, to be succeeded by Gamal Abdel Nasser and his new republic.

Above Young men and boys staring into the camera in Alexandria, probably in the early 1920s. Alexandria is the chief port of Egypt and was a major base for British forces.

Left Egyptian *dhows* in the Nile in the 1920s. The Nile is the lifeblood of Egypt and journeys on the river, to see the sites of ancient Egypt, became one of the great colonial adventures.

Left The great pyramid of Khephren at Giza, taken in 1913. The pyramid of Khephren is the second pyramid at Giza, slightly smaller (2.5 metres) than the great pyramid of Khufu nearby.

Below A camel journey by two British women at Bi-Hareen, Egypt, probably in the 1920s. For intrepid British travellers, an "expedition" along the Nile to Egypt's great wonders was the journey of a lifetime for the few who could afford it. The fact that the journey could be conducted under the protection of the British flag was a great comfort to those anxious about the trip.

Above The pyramids at Giza, taken in 1913. The pyramid of Khufu is in the foreground, Khephren in the middle and the smaller pyramid of Menkaure in the distance.

Right An exotic journey for a British couple in Egypt in the 1920s. Holidays like this were for the privileged few and rarely undertaken during this period. Photographs to record their adventures, especially in colour, were even more unusual.

Left A British woman taking a camel ride in Egypt, in the 1920s. She is doubly protected from the Egyptian sun by a hat and parasol, but modesty prevents her wearing anything less than her voluminous skirt.

Right The Colossi of Memnon, *circa* 1920. Egyptians with camels pose in front of the two huge statues of Amenhotep III (1390–52BC) in western Thebes.

Above A visitor relaxes at the Temple of Isis at Philae, Egypt, in 1913. Philae's island setting was a romantic attraction for nineteenth-century visitors. But the building of the first Aswan Dam (1902) meant that much of it was submerged for part of the year. The temples were later dismantled and rebuilt on the nearby island of Agilkia.

Left The same visitor, resting with an Egyptian guide beneath the walls of a large temple or pyramid, 1913. Probably the Temple of Isis at Philae, as above.

JERUSALEM

Jerusalem, the holy city of Judaism, Christianity and Islam, was the capital city of the British-mandated territory of Palestine from the end of the First World War until it relinquished its mandate to the United Nations in 1948. Prior to British control, Palestine had been a part of the Ottoman Empire for almost seven hundred years.

Above Jerusalem's Golden Gate during the 1920s. By declaring its sympathy with the Zionist dream of a Jewish homeland in Palestine (in the 1917 statement of British Foreign Secretary Arthur Balfour – the Balfour Declaration), British rule meant that increasing numbers of Jews migrated to their ancestral homeland during the 1920s and 1930s.

Left Women and children on the steps of a temple in an unknown location (possibly Burma) between *circa* 1915.

FOREIGN TRAVEL

The sheer scale of Britain's empire offered a remarkably diverse range of exotic locations for travel and adventure, but only to those who could afford it. For the less well-off, travel to strange lands was still possible, but hardship, danger, fatigue or disease were often the price for the thousands of soldiers, administrators, nurses, teachers and missionaries who took up the imperial challenge.

Right The fruit of the Orient, *circa* 1920. A young boy displays a freshly cut fruit for the camera. Burma is a possible location.

Left Elephant labour, *circa* 1920. Elephants were used as labour throughout the Empire, but especially in India, Ceylon and Burma, and in particular in the logging industry.

Above A Buddhist priest in the garden of his temple, Burma, 1914.

Right Two Burmese women resting during their plantation work, *circa* 1920. They may well be working on a tea plantation.

Right Hong Kong Harbour
around the time of the First
World War. Hong Kong island
was ceded to Britain by China
in 1842 and became the great
outpost of the Empire in the Far
East. But in the early days of
the century it was a far more
modest version of the metropolis
it would later become.

THE SECOND WORLD WAR

The Second World War was in many ways the last hurrah of the British Empire. The inevitability of the demise of British imperial power was already determined long before war broke out, and most British colonies would win their independence within two decades of the end of the war. But the economic strength and manpower of the Empire was a vital third element, with the United States and the Soviet Union, in the Grand Alliance's fight against Germany and Japan.

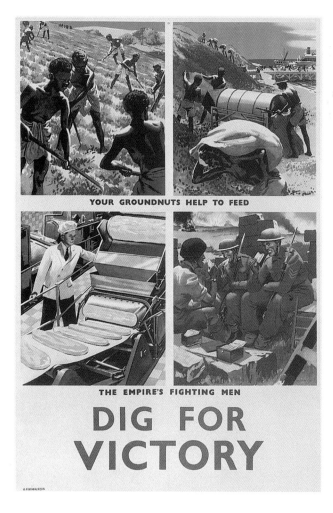

Above A "Dig For Victory" poster for the African colonies, 1940. As in the First World War, Britain and her Empire fought as one in the Second World War and, in many cases, endured similar hardships on the domestic front.

Above An armed forces recruitment poster from the Second World War. Empire forces during the war included the following contingents:

Great Britain	4,650,000
India	1,789,000
Canada	770,000
Australia	570,000
East African colonies	255,000
West African colonies	166,000
New Zealand	97,000

CULTURAL DIVISIONS

The unity of intent, which typified the attitude of Empire servicemen called to arms during the Second World War, was, in large part, a firm response to a frightening foe. After the foe was vanquished, the unity of intent evaporated. Many soldiers of the white Commonwealth realized that, although many of them were kith and kin of their British cousins, large differences of culture had developed over the years. Similarly, men from Africa, Asia and the Caribbean discovered that, although their labour and force of arms were valued, they were unlikely to be treated as equals by their British officers or supervisors.

Above The British prime minister, Winston Churchill, William Mackenzie King, the prime minister of Canada, the Earl of Athlone, Governor-General of Canada and the United States president, Franklin D. Roosevelt, on the terrace of the citadel in Quebec, Canada, August 1943. The four men were attending the first Ottawa Conference at which the strategy for the Normandy landings was agreed.

Right Commonwealth Joint Air Training Plan, No. 23 Air School, Waterkloof, Pretoria, South Africa, January 1943. Group Captain Dalzell leads an RAF pipe band.

Above British officers relaxing in Africa in 1942.

SOUTH AFRICA

South Africa played a significant part in the war effort, despite considerable opposition from the Afrikaans-speaking community, many of whom still resented British actions during the Boer War and the gradual Anglicization of the country following it. However, over 330,000 South Africans volunteered for service, including over 120,000 black South Africans. South African casualties during the war amounted to more than 9,000 dead.

Left Basuto "hanger boys" clean and polish a Miles Master 2036 training plane at Kumalo near Bulawayo, January 1943.

Right The RAF in West Africa, March 1943. The Air Officer commanding Royal Air Force, West African Command, Air Vice-Marshal J.B. Cole-Hamilton.

Opposite A proud soldier, with his assegai shouldered, stands guard at No. 23 Air School, Waterkloof, Pretoria, January 1943.

Above A crew of No. 200 Squadron with a camera about to board a Hudson "K-King" for an anti-submarine patrol being helped by local workers (March 1943).

COLONIAL CONTRIBUTION

Although there was what amounted to a colour bar in the British armed forces during the Second World War, it is estimated that more than 370,000 Africans were recruited into largely non-combat roles. Of these, it is suggested that at least 7,000 died. It is also thought that of the 30,000 British merchant seamen who died during the war, 5,000 were of colonial origin. By 1943, the RAF had decided to recruit 6,400 West Indians, of whom 800 served as aircrew.

Above A Colonial Rest Centre, England, 1944. Dr A.H. Cadinouche from Mauritius, a doctor whose peacetime practice was in Paris, reads a copy of the *Illustrated London News*. Dr Cadinouche would almost certainly have been involved in helping fatigued soldiers with their recuperation.

Above A group of students and members of the Auxiliary Territorial Service from the British colonies at a Colonial Rest Centre in England, in 1944.

CEYLON

Ceylon was an important strategic location for the Empire and the Allies during the Second World War. The island suffered a heavy attack from the aircraft of a major Japanese naval task force in April 1942, but saw no more action. In June 1944, Kandy became the headquarters of South East Asia Command.

Above A Servicemen's Leave Camp, Kandy, November 1944. Service personnel relaxing and taking elephant rides at the Mahaveli Ganga river.

Above A paradise of rest and recuperation amid the stress and danger of war. British servicemen and servicewomen at the exotic Mount Lavinia Beach, Ceylon, January 1945.

INDIA

India's men, resources and strategic location were of enormous importance to the war effort during the Second World War. The Indian Army fought in Italy, Greece, North and East Africa, Syria, Iraq, Malaya and in very large numbers in Burma. By the end of the war, India had more than 2.5 million men under arms. It was also implicit in the agreement between Britain and India that the latter's support of the Allied cause would guarantee Indian independence after the war had ended.

Above Lord and Lady Wavell in the Mogul Gardens, Viceroy House, New Delhi, February 1945. Archibald Wavell had fought in the Boer War and the First World War and had been Commander-in-Chief, Middle East Command in 1939. He was appointed Viceroy of India in October 1943 and was succeeded by Lord Louis Mountbatten in 1945.

Right Three WAAFs (Women's Auxiliary Air Force) sightseeing at the Secretariat Building, New Delhi, February 1945.

Opposite Troops buying fruit from a street vendor in the grounds of the Viceroy's House, New Delhi, February 1945. New Delhi replaced Calcutta as India's capital in 1912.

Above Lord Wavell, the Viceroy, inspects his state carriage (February 1945). Wavell would soon be replaced by Lord Louis Mountbatten.

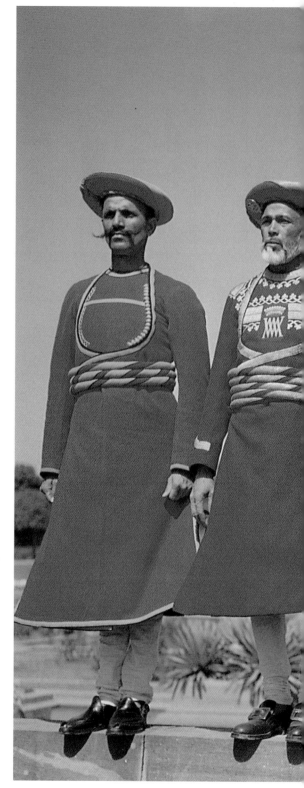

Right Very finely dressed servants and a young messenger boy (barefooted) at the Viceroy's House, New Delhi, March 1945. The Viceregal House, designed by Sir Edwin Lutyens, was completed in 1930.

BURMA

There were over 71,000 British and Commonwealth casualties during the campaign in Burma. In 1944, Lord Mountbatten praised these soldiers along with "a small force of British and Indian troops, under Brigadier Wingate" who captured the imagination of the world when they made the first experiment in long range penetration and proved that they could outwit and outfight the Japanese.

Left Hoisting the Union Jack at Fort Dufferin, during the Battle of Mandalay, March 1945. It was a victory for General Sir William Slim's 14th Army.

Opposite British troops resting in front of a colourful Buddha on Pagoda Hill along the road to Mandalay, Burma, March 1945.

Above The investiture of five Victoria Crosses, awarded to members of the Indian Army for their valour during the Second World War. New Delhi, March 1945.

A NEW BRITAIN

Although Britain had always had strong, multicultural elements due to its Empire and large volume of trade with other countries, the Second World War was a watershed of political and economic change. It led to rapid postwar decolonization and, ultimately, to a new, multicultural Britain that reflected its imperial history.

Below Muslims in Britain during the Second World War. A Muslim procession toward a new Mosque and cultural centre, Butetown, Cardiff, 1943.

1944–1967
THE WIND OF CHANGE

In her three-volume history of the rise and decline of the British Empire, Jan Morris described the efforts of Britain and her Empire during the Second World War as "a grand performance in noble purpose, a swan song of some splendour, and a worthy last display of imperial brotherhood". And so it was.

In 1940, Britain acquired a new prime minister, a man who would not only embody all that the British needed to find in themselves, but also all that emanated from its imperial past. Winston Churchill conducted the war with the authority and arrogance of a man who had "lived" the Empire. He had fought at Omdurman, on the North West Frontier and on the Western Front; he had witnessed the Boer War and had been imprisoned by the enemy; he had been First Sea Lord in the Great War and Minister of War; he had even taken the blame for the disastrous campaign in the Dardanelles and thus understood the price to be paid in conflict. Churchill would be not just British Prime Minister but the Commander in Chief of a vast imperial army, navy and airforce, the like of which would have enthralled Nelson, Clive and Wolfe, let alone his own illustrious ancestor, John Churchill, the first Duke of Marlborough.

There were many examples of heroism in the spirit of the Empire. The island of Malta withstood a two-and-a-half-year siege and long periods of continuous bombardment, during which most of the island's buildings were destroyed, to become a symbol of the resolve that typified the Empire's spirit. Malta's almost farcically meagre air defence – three biplanes called *Faith*, *Hope* and *Charity* – became the stuff of legends, both a propaganda boost and real hope and inspiration. When, in August 1942, Malta was finally on its knees, with little food, water or fuel left, a remarkable feat of naval heroics saved the day. In Operation Pedestal, the British Navy despatched a force of 44 warships, including three aircraft carriers, two battleships and seven cruisers, in order to force through 14 merchant navy supply ships. Amid a massive onslaught of enemy fire, only five of the merchantmen got through to unload their precious supplies. The garrison survived and, in a unique gesture, the entire island was awarded the newly instituted George Cross for bravery. King George VI travelled to Malta in 1943 to bestow the medal in person.

There were fewer heroic redoubts in the Far East. Some positions were impossible to defend; perhaps in truth, Singapore was one of them, but the ease with which it fell sent a shock wave throughout the Empire and the world, especially in the Far East, India, Australia and New Zealand. The squadrons of planes and fleet of warships, promised to the dominions in 1937, never materialized (except the token and ill-fated gesture of the battleship *Prince of Wales* and the cruiser *Repulse*). The strategic defence of the island had always assumed an attack from the sea. Singapore's narrow strait to the north, separating it from the Malaysian peninsula, was seriously exposed. Preparations for the defence of the island were a shambles, even when the Japanese arrived within sight of the city. Surely, it was thought, this race of small men, with their exaggerated bowing and strange ceremonies, could do little to damage the might of Britain's strategic pivot in Asia!

Churchill demanded that the city be defended "to the death". He said that Britain's military reputation and "the honour of the Empire" were at stake. "There was to be no thought of surrender." But Churchill and Britain were far away. The worst nightmare of conquering peoples followed: the worst kind of military humiliation for those who would claim innate superiority; the worst kind of abject defeat: the garrison at Singapore surrendered with barely a whimper. Detached assessment suggests that General Arthur Percival was right not to sacrifice thousands of civilians in a futile fight. Nonetheless, at the time, and in the deep and murky recesses of imperial pride, it was a disaster of monumental proportions. It was also one of those moments, like Amritsar, when sage observers thought they had seen the death throes of the Empire.

But the war was won, and when it was over there followed a short interlude that allowed a brief glimpse of former glory. For, despite the power of Britain's partners in the Grand Alliance – the United States and the Soviet Union – Britain, as joint victor in the great conflict, not only retained its huge empire but also held temporary domain as lords of its vanquished enemies, Germany and Japan. Thus, for a moment, before sovereignty was restored, Britain's sphere of influence was greater than ever before and covered vast swathes of Europe, the Mediterranean and the Pacific. But it was the last gleaming of the twilight of the Empire.

Once again Australians, New Zealanders, Canadians and South Africans had shed their blood for the mother country. The rest of the Empire had also made massive commitments of men and resources. Their blood was shed for their white rulers. In the years to come, each part of the Empire would choose its own route for the future.

The Second World War had led, inevitably, to a continuing delay in solving the problem of India. A solution had to be found and, sooner or later, that solution would mean independence. But the dilemma was, how? The subcontinent was so large and diverse that it didn't seem possible. The issue of 90 million Muslims was the most difficult of all. They wanted their own state, so independence might mean two nations and the terrifying prospect of partition. Intercommunal violence was getting worse, thousands were dying. In London, Churchill's vision, so clear in wartime, was clouded in peacetime. He refused to surrender the jewel in the crown.

But Churchill lost the 1945 general election to the Labour Party. Clement Attlee, the new prime minister, had a clear view of the way forward in India. He appointed a new viceroy, Lord Louis Mountbatten, a great-grandson of the original Queen-Empress herself, Queen Victoria. He was one of the war's warrior-leaders and the ideal figure to ensure that the British would leave their precious Raj with dignity. Attlee and Mountbatten finally grasped the nettle: they set a date for independence – no later than June 1948.

As all politicians do, even ones seconded from a Royal family and distinguished service in the military, Mountbatten wrote his own history and managed events so that they best reflected his role in them. But even so, the new viceroy's achievements were remarkable. He talked openly and frankly to Indians, embracing them and insisting that they make preparations for self-determination in ways that would make future generations of the new nation feel proud. No imperial representative had ever before spoken with them like this.

Mountbatten's discussion with the three main Indian leaders – Gandhi, the spiritual leader and, by 1947, the elder statesman of the Indian National Congress, Jawaharlal Nehru, the Congress's foremost political voice, and Muhammed Ali Jinnah, the leader of the putative state of Pakistan – led him to conclude that partition to create a separate Muslim state was unavoidable; and that it must happen soon. Mountbatten made the announcement himself; the date of independence would be advanced to August 15, 1947. After 250 years of British presence in India, they would be gone in just 73 days.

Like a stack of cards, generations of passion and dreams came tumbling down. All the detail which makes an empire memorable – a level paved road, a small, smart classroom, a beautifully kept churchyard – were as nothing. It was right that it should be so, but painful to bear for those who had built them. For the Indians and Pakistanis who were to inherit this new land, there was the realization of decades of hope to savour, and the horror of immediate anarchy to endure. At least 200,000 people died in the ensuing violence as Hindus migrated to the new India and Muslims moved to the new Pakistan. But it was done; the Raj was cut loose, the end had begun.

Britain now began to contemplate the end of its Empire, attempting to approach it in a new and optimistic manner. It had created a new concept intended to enthuse both its white cousins in the dominions and its black friends in its great imperial diaspora: not an empire of ruler and ruled, but a Commonwealth of Nations, a consensual collective of diverse peoples, sharing common traditions, beliefs and values.

This shift of emphasis, a sort of cultural reinvention, added a new vigour to postwar Britain. In 1953, the Royal Family delivered a new pageant to symbolize the future: a new, young queen, Elizabeth II. She would herald a second Elizabethan Age and was immediately despatched on a grand tour of the Commonwealth. The tour kept traditional loyalties alive, but Canada, Australia and New Zealand continued gradually to formulate their own destinies. In South Africa, the die was cast. After half a century of continuity, a sea change in South African politics meant that a new nationalist, Afrikaner government would take the country down the catastrophic road of racial segregation to Apartheid. Eventually, its perverse solution to a multiracial society – oppression disguised as "separate development" – would result in it leaving the Commonwealth in 1961.

But before the Commonwealth of Nations could be made real, there were many more peoples around the world who demanded to be granted the rite of passage to nationhood. First of all, the situation in one of Britain's thorniest inheritances – Palestine – had to be resolved. This was not to be Britain's finest hour. The events of the Second World War, and the horrible fate to which Adolf Hitler had attempted to consign the Jewish people, had rendered all of Britain's prewar successes in maintaining a delicate peace in Palestine a distant memory. Unable to curb a growing Jewish revolt,

Britain abandoned its mandate, admitting that the land was ungovernable. As the British scurried away in 1948, the triumphant Zionists seized their chance and the new state of Israel was born.

In Malaya, the new British "Empire of the mind" – the great Commonwealth of people wedded to Anglo-Saxon liberal democracy – faced the new threat of the postwar world: the communism of the Cold War. They faced it resolutely, defeated Malaya's communist rebels and succeeded in allowing the new Malaysian federation to begin life amid relative order. Wider ideological and strategic issues also played a significant role in another salutary lesson for Britain – the Suez Crisis.

The British presence in the Middle East was becoming unpalatable for the Egyptian leadership, whose increasing radicalism reflected the growing significance of demands for self-determination and independence throughout the world. Egypt also had Gamal Abdel Nasser, a leader whose charisma roused Arab consciousness all over the Middle East. For Anthony Eden, the new prime minister, it seemed as if the ghost of Italy's dictator Benito Mussolini had come back to haunt the British (Eden had resigned as Foreign Secretary in 1938 because of Neville Chamberlain's decision to negotiate with Mussolini over the Italian invasion of Abyssinia). Appeasing dictators had failed in 1938 and Eden was not prepared to do it again.

Britain also resented the fact that, as its power in the Mediterranean and Near East began to wane, the power of the United States replaced it. Although a nation of cousins and allies, America was a brash, upstart country, appearing, in the eyes of many in Britain, to lack the finesse and manners of a great power. So when, in July 1956, Nasser nationalized the Suez Canal Company, seizing British and Western assets, Eden decided to make a stand. But Britain was divided: the old war-horses of Empire yearned for a fight to teach the Egyptians a lesson; more modern liberals pleaded for caution. With hindsight, it may have seemed like Munich, but these were different men and different circumstances.

In October, following a deal brokered by the French, Britain's very willing allies in the crisis, the Israelis, invaded Egypt across the Sinai Desert in a surprise attack. The ruse presented Britain and France with the perfect opportunity to occupy Egyptian territory, using the excuse that they were protecting the strategic importance of the Canal against the two combatants. RAF Canberra bombers attacked Egyptian targets and the invasion began in earnest in early November. Militarily, the operation was a resounding success, but in Britain there was a row of huge proportions about the ethics involved. In the end, money rather than ethics brought the crisis to an end. Britain's economy was struggling and it had applied to the International Monetary Fund for a loan. The Americans, who controlled the IMF, would not sanction it unless Anglo-French troops were withdrawn from the Suez region. There was no choice but to accede. Another of those seminal moments had happened. The world drew its own conclusions. The Conservative MP Angus Maude suggested that Britain should "admit to the world that we are now an American satellite".

The humiliation of Suez cost Anthony Eden his job. He was replaced as prime minister by Harold Macmillan. Under Macmillan's leadership, from 1957 to 1963, the greater part of the remaining British Empire disappeared. A dozen countries, mainly in Africa, won their independence and plans for several more were put firmly into place.

The exotic-sounding Gold Coast was the first, in 1957, renaming itself Ghana. The new country's leader, Kwame Nkrumah, had evoked the full spectrum of views from the colonial administration; initially dismissed as the country's very own Adolf Hitler, he was finally seen as Africa's best hope. In time, the hope turned to despair, as Nkrumah abandoned democracy and was eventually removed in a coup.

In Kenya, the hopes of British settlers that it might remain a white man's land were rendered futile by an armed revolt by the Kikuyu tribe – the Mau Mau rebellion. For a while, a vicious struggle ensued but, inevitably, Jomo Kenyatta, the leader of Kenya's nationalist movement, whom the British had imprisoned, was released and became the new leader of the country when it won independence in 1963.

Macmillan travelled to Africa in 1960 to see for himself the changes which were transforming the continent. When he spoke to the South African parliament, he uttered the famous words that encapsulated the sudden reality of Britain's Empire in Africa. He intended his message as an appeal to the continent's white settlers to embrace pragmatism and accept the inevitable. After likening Britain's imperial demise to the end of the Roman Empire, he said: "The wind of change is blowing through this continent and, whether we like it or not, this growth of national consciousness is a political fact. We must all accept it is a fact and our policies must take account of it." In the next few years, Britain granted independence to most of its colonies in Africa and the Caribbean.

Macmillan's pragmatism, in accepting Britain's fate, was perhaps more telling than the recent succession of independence celebrations in symbolizing the end of the Empire, for the founders of the Empire were not pragmatists, they were dreamers. Not all of their dreams were entirely laudable, nor were many of them realized without intolerance and cruelty, but, nonetheless, they were dreamers. And now the dream seemed to be over.

INDIA

Independence for India came suddenly, dramatically and tragically. After nearly three centuries, during which Britain tried to forge unity in the subcontinent, Muslim fears of being dominated by Hindus led to the new state being partitioned between a secular India and a Muslim Pakistan. More than 500,000 people died in the communal violence that followed.

Left The Secretariat, New Delhi, 1945. This was the administrative heart of the Raj, the place from where, the British proudly boasted, just a few thousand civil servants successfully ruled a diverse land of many hundreds of millions.

Right Lord Louis Mountbatten, the last Viceroy of India, working at his desk in New Delhi, 1947. As the great-grandson of Queen Victoria, the great Empress of the Raj, it was perhaps appropriate that he should oversee the process of Indian independence.

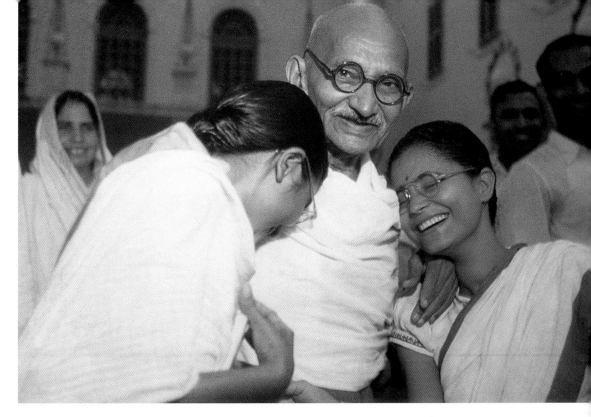

Right Mahatma Gandhi with his granddaughters at Binka House, New Delhi (*circa* 1947). Gandhi became the father of the Indian nation and a spiritual leader of non-violent political reform throughout the world. His personal fasts, imploring people to desist from acts of violence, may well have averted even more bloodshed during the violence of partition. In 1948, Gandhi was assassinated by a Hindu extremist.

Above Jawaharlal Nehru, prime minister of India 1947–64, was imprisoned for long periods during the last days of British rule. As president of the Indian National Congress, he became the nation's first leader after independence (1946).

Above Muhammed Ali Jinnah was instrumental in backing the policy of peaceful coexistence between Muslims and Hindus. However, by 1940 he was advocating a separate state for India's Muslims in Pakistan, one that he led when it was granted independence from a partitioned India in 1947.

ROYAL TOUR OF SOUTH AFRICA

In 1947, King George VI and Queen Elizabeth visited South Africa as part of a royal tour of Africa. The South African prime minister, Jan Smuts, had supported Britain during the Second World War and was an advocate of strong ties with Britain. It was hoped that the visit would reinforce traditional loyalties to Britain and the Empire. However, after Smuts lost the general election to the Nationalist Party in 1948, they introduced a policy of Apartheid, which led to South Africa leaving the Commonwealth in 1961.

Right The King and Queen, acknowledging the large crowds at a football stadium in Port Elizabeth, 1947.

Left Expectant crowds at the border of Basutoland (which became Lesotho in 1966) and the South African Orange Free State province awaiting the royal visit, 1947.

Left Dignitaries awaiting the royal couple, the royal tour of South Africa, 1947. From the right: Sir Evelyn Baring, High Commissioner of Bechuanaland, Basutoland and Swaziland; Lieutenant-Colonel A. Forsyth-Thompson; Mantsebo Seeiso, Head Chief of Basutoland and, on the left, her interpreter.

Right Paramount Chief Batheon of the Bangwakatse tribe. Resplendent in a plumed helmet and scarlet tunic, reminiscent of the Life Guards, the chief presented an address of welcome to the king on his arrival at Lobatsi, Bechuanaland, 1947. His colleague is another chief, whose uniform bears a striking resemblance to that of the Blues and Royals.

LIFE IN THE COLONIES

For many colonial officials, service personnel and administrators, life in the colonies could be both very enjoyable and rewarding. Very often, a relaxed way of life was possible in an exhilarating climate. But life could also be very demanding, lonely and occasionally dangerous. Although some climates were a blessing, others could be a curse, and fatigue and disease were commonplace.

Above Fun under a tropical sky, Singapore Swimming Club 1947. Singapore was part of the Federation of Malaya when it was granted independence in 1948, but became a separate sovereign state in 1965.

Above An idyllic setting at Bermuda's Coral
Beach Club, 1947. Bermuda became a Crown
Colony in 1684 and has remained staunchly
British ever since.

THE COMMONWEALTH

The British sovereign has always been both the head of state for all Britain's imperial possessions and the embodiment of the Empire. Britain's first Elizabethan Age saw the foundation of a future Empire built on the strength of the English Navy. Around 350 years later, it was hoped that a new Queen Elizabeth would be able to rule over a new British Commonwealth of Nations.

Below Queen Elizabeth II and her consort, the Duke of Edinburgh, posing for official photographs following her coronation in 1953.

Right The Queen and the royal family on tour, 1954. Late in 1953 the Queen undertook a major tour of her Empire and Commonwealth. The island of Malta was visited towards the end of the tour, in May 1954. A young Princess Anne and Prince Charles are greeted by the governor, Gerald Creasey, as they go ashore.

Above The royal yacht *Britannia*, in the foreground, protected by the cruisers *Glasgow* and *Gambia* of the Mediterranean Fleet of the Royal Navy. Valetta harbour, Malta, 1954.

Above Australian children wave enthusiastically as the royal couple
pass by in 1954. Throughout the royal tour, thousands of people
clamoured to see the new queen. Part of the success of the tour must
have reflected the glamour of a new queen, but it must also have been
a celebration of the fact that Britain and the Empire had survived the
war. It confirmed that the traditional ties to Britain still meant
something to millions of people across the world.

Above Nine-year-old Janette Kurr presents a golden basket of flowers to the Queen outside the town hall of Wollongong, New South Wales during the royal tour of Australia in 1954. More than 80,000 people lined the streets to see the Queen.

Above The Queen and the Duke of Edinburgh watch a cattle round-up at Hamilton Downs Cattle Station near Alice Springs during the royal tour, 1954.

THE SUEZ CRISIS

In 1956, Britain and its ally France launched a military attack on the Suez Canal zone in Egypt in order to try and protect its interests there after the Egyptian leader, President Nasser, had nationalized the Canal and thus brought it under Egyptian control. When the United States refused to support Britain's position, British forces had to make an embarrassing withdrawal. Many commentators have said that the Suez Crisis was a turning point in British imperial history; a point beyond which Britain could no longer exercise the kind of authority on the international stage that it had been previously been able to.

Right Troops from the United Nations Peacekeeping Force arrive in Port Said in November 1956. The UN force ensured stability in the region, especially in the context of fighting between Egypt and its neighbour Israel in the Sinai desert, which had sparked the Suez Crisis.

CARIBBEAN TERRITORIES

Most of the islands of the Caribbean became part of the British Empire in the eighteenth century. Sugar became the economic base of the colonies, grown on plantations that were cultivated by slaves from Africa. It is estimated that during the 1780s 350,000 slaves were shipped from Africa by the British and that the figure was 420,000 in the 1790s.

Right Station Sergeant L.O. Primus, Drill Instructor for the police on St Vincent in the Windward Islands, March 1955. He wears the 1939–45 war ribbon, having served as a member of the local armed forces during the Second World War.

Opposite A young schoolboy, Nathaniel Pemberton, climbing a flagpole with its Union Jack at Molineux School on St Kitts in the Leeward Islands, March 1955. The school was built in 1948 by the United Kingdom Colonial Development Welfare Fund.

Left 23-year-old Marie David inspects tobacco plants to remove offshoots, caterpillars and worms at the Hillsborough Tobacco Estate on Dominica in the Windward Islands, March 1955. Tobacco and coffee were additional products planted to support the sugar industry.

Below Men of HQ Company 1st East Anglia Regiment inspect the fruit and vegetables at Bourda Market, British Guiana, January 1963.

Opposite The British Army on peacekeeping duties in British Guiana. A patrol of the Lancashire Fusiliers, sporting their bright yellow hackles, set out in canoes from their base in the jungle, watched by local children, May 1965. Ethnic conflict, between the majority population of Indian descent and the minority of African descent, marred much of the 1960s. In 1966, the country became the independent nation of Guyana.

EAST AFRICA

British possessions in East Africa were pioneered at the end of the nineteenth century and became defined as British East Africa (Kenya), Uganda and Zanzibar. After the First World War, the former German territory of Tanganyika became part of the British Empire.

Left The District Commissioner of Bagamoyo Bomo, Tanganyika, Major John Piper, relaxing on the East African coast with his friends and young daughter, *circa* 1955.

Right Major Piper's daughter, Lesley, on the veranda of the Pipers' family home in Tanganyika, *circa* 1955.

Left Major John Piper on safari in Tanganyika, *circa* 1955.

Below Elephant tusks confiscated from poachers by the government, *circa* 1955. Then as now, poaching was a major threat to African wildlife.

Left Villagers dance to celebrate their new dam filling with water, Sukumaland, Tanganyika, *circa* 1955. The new dam reduced the distance to be walked to collect water from an average of seven miles to three.

Right A bridge being built across the river at Kimbe, Tanganyika, *circa* 1955.

Right Francis
Townsend and his
askari (Arabic for
"soldier/policeman")
listening to the
arguments in a
border dispute
between the Masai
and Handeni,
Tanganyika, *circa*
1955.

Above A guard of honour outside the district commission of Kisarawe District, Tanganyika, *circa* 1955.

Right Government House, Dar es Salaam, Tanganyika, *circa* 1960. Tanganyika became the independent republic of Tanzania in 1961. Zanzibar, which became independent in 1963, merged with Tanzania in 1964.

Above Schoolchildren holding Union Jacks, as they await
the royal yacht *Britannia*, carrying Princess Margaret on her
royal tour of East Africa, October 9, 1956.

Above British officials and local dignitaries on their way to open the Sessions of the Courts in Zanzibar, 1956. British rule in Zanzibar operated indirectly, through the support of the local sultan.

Left British ship HMS *Ceylon* anchored off the coast of Zanzibar, 1956. Despite its continuing presence in the waters of the world, the power of the Royal Navy was waning fast after the Second World War.

Below Three British officers lean on the rail of their ship.

Above A netball match in progress at a primary
school near Kampala, Uganda, *circa* 1950. Sport,
especially those sports codified and spread by
the British – football, rugby and cricket –
became an important part of the culture of the
Empire.

Left A spiral casing for the No. 3 generator being installed in the hydroelectric power plant, as the Owen Falls Dam project nears completion, Jinja, Uganda, *circa* 1954. One of hundreds of engineering projects undertaken throughout Africa under British rule.

Right A BOAC Comet at Entebbe Airport, Uganda (1950s). The jet is en route from London to Johannesburg. Trade and communications had always been vital to the functioning of the Empire, but air travel transformed the speed of communications and "shrank" the scale of the Empire.

Left Mr Dick Mason, farmer and settler in the Mau-Narok area of Kenya, talks to his Kikuyu tractor driver, during the last days of the bloody Mau Mau uprising: a land dispute between the white settlers of Kenya's Aberdare Mountains and the traditional owners, the Kikuyu tribe.

Below Tea company lorries being loaded for export to the Sudan (1950s).

Above Masai boys and teachers standing outside the first boarding school in Masai country at Kajiado, Kenya (1950s). Boarding schools made sense to the colonial British, but less so to the Masai, a fiercely independent nomadic people.

Left A piper of the 1st Battalion Gordon Highlanders, meeting a warrior in full battle dress in East Africa, 1963.

Above *Askaris* of the Kenyan police force on parade with their Sikh officer at Kisumu police station, Kenya in the 1950s. Many Asians settled in East Africa under British rule. Most left countries like Kenya and Uganda after independence in the face of hostility and discrimination.

Left The governor of Kenya, Sir Philip Mitchell, talking to Masai warriors waiting at Nairobi Airport to greet the royal party on their tour of Kenya in 1952. Both the governor and the Masai look impressive in their feather headdresses.

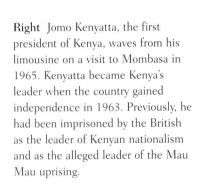

Right Jomo Kenyatta, the first president of Kenya, waves from his limousine on a visit to Mombasa in 1965. Kenyatta became Kenya's leader when the country gained independence in 1963. Previously, he had been imprisoned by the British as the leader of Kenyan nationalism and as the alleged leader of the Mau Mau uprising.

WEST AFRICA

British territories in West Africa, which included Gambia, Sierra Leone, Gold Coast and Nigeria, were consolidated after some wrangling with the French – who also had significant interests in West Africa – at the end of the nineteenth century. Adventurers like George Taubman Goldie and Frederick Lugard pioneered British interests in the region in the grand imperial style: a potent combination of charismatic bravery and personal aggrandisement.

Above Girls being taught by a nun at a convent school in Bo, Sierra Leone in the 1950s. Among the Africans is a Lebanese girl. Sierra Leone became independent in 1961. Its capital, Freetown, had been founded as a haven for freed slaves in 1787 and became a colony of the British Crown in 1808.

Above The Chief of Osino in the Ashanti area of the Gold Coast, West Africa, receives a report from a British agricultural officer, surrounded by the Chief's elders, *circa* 1950. The report concerns an outbreak of "swollen shoot", a disease of cocoa plants. At this time cocoa was a vital crop of the area, so such outbreaks were of major concern.

Opposite Schoolchildren marching at a parade watched over by Dr Taylor-Cummings, the mayor of Freetown, Sierra Leone, 1951. The parade was part of Sierra Leone's Empire Day celebrations, but was held in February because the weather in May, during the country's rainy season, would have been unsuitable.

Above Women of Illiassa in the Gambia, drawing water at a well that has been cleared and given a concrete surround by the district authority, *circa* 1950. Gambia was part of the Empire from 1888 until its independence in 1965. Gambia's capital, Banjul (known as Bathurst in the period of British rule), was established as a base for British anti-slavery operations in 1816.

Right Shark fillets spread out to dry in the sun at the shore station of Atlantic Fisheries (the Colonial Development Corporation's fishing project) in the Gambia, *circa* 1950.

Above The Gold Coast Regiment on parade through the streets of Accra, Gold Coast, 1956. The following year the Gold Coast became the independent nation of Ghana under its first leader, Kwame Nkrumah. The Gold Coast had been part of the Empire since 1874.

Right The royal tour of Ghana, 1961. The Queen and the Duke of Edinburgh are presented to chiefs of the Central Region at a durbar in Victoria Park, Cape Coast.

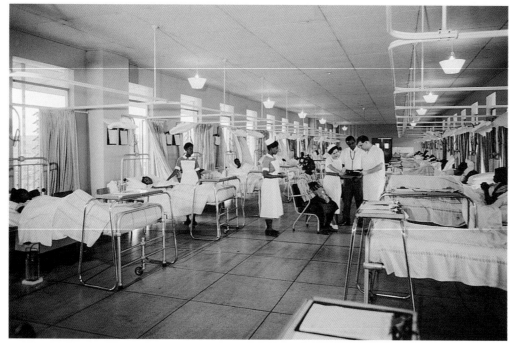

Below Two doctors discuss a patient's progress with a ward sister and a student nurse at University College Training Hospital, Ibadan, Nigeria (1959). Nigeria was Britain's largest colony in Africa and was brought under British control in stages, until completion in 1906. It became independent in 1960.

Left A portrait of Alaki of Abeokuta, chief of the Yoruba people of Nigeria, (1958). British control in West Africa was founded on indirect rule through the traditional aristocracy of tribal leaders.

Right Dignitaries in their finery, both traditional African and traditional British, at Nigeria's Independence Day celebrations in Lagos in 1961.

SOUTH-EAST ASIA

British possessions in South East Asia reflected the ambitions of men like Stamford Raffles and Sir James Brooke. Raffles acquired Singapore island in 1819 and Brooke, through remarkable audacity, became "Rajah" of Sarawak in 1841. Ultimately, these territories became amalgamated as Malaya.

Above The Sultan of Kelantan with the Crown Prince on his right. Mr W.F.N. Churchill, British advisor to the Sultan, stands on his left, Malaya (1950s). As in so many parts of the Empire, indirect rule was essential to British governance.

Transporting supplies on a dockside in Malaya in 1965. Malaya became an independent federation in 1957.

Right Cricket, that most English of games, being played on the Padang (playing field) at Kuantan, Malaya in the 1950s. Cricket didn't captivate the Malaysians, but it became central to life on the Indian subcontinent and in the Caribbean.

Left Neat rows of schoolchildren on parade at a fête in Semporna, North Borneo (Sabah) in the 1950s. Sabah is part of the island of Borneo, separated from the mainland of Malaya by over four hundred miles.

Right A platoon commander of the 1st Battalion Royal Green Jackets, discussing positions to be manned by the unit near Sapit in Sarawak, July 1964. From 1948 a communist-inspired uprising against British rule led to ten years of guerrilla war on the mainland. After independence, raids into Sarawak on the island of Borneo, from neighbouring Indonesia, led British forces to be employed in the Borneo Campaign until it ended in 1966.

Above Two members of a patrol of the Royal Ulster Rifles are entertained in an Iban longhouse in Sarawak during the Borneo Campaign, July 1964. A successful "hearts and minds" policy had been pioneered by the British during the Malayan Emergency in the 1950s. It was used to great effect again in Borneo.

Above Two soldiers of the Queen's Own Highlanders on guard in the Seria oilfields, Brunei, January 1963. The troops were in Seria to rescue Europeans who had been captured by local rebels and held prisoner in a police station for three days.

Right A boat patrol of the Queen's Own Highlanders, searching for rebels in the area around Seria, January 1963.

SINGAPORE

After its development by Sir Stamford Raffles, Singapore became the most important trading centre for Britain's empire in South East Asia. It became a Crown Colony in 1867. Although it became part of the Federation of Malaysia upon independence in 1963, it broke away in 1965 to become an independent republic.

Below A music lesson in progress at the school for Gurkha children at Slim Barracks, Singapore, the home of the 2nd Battalion, 2nd King Edward VII's Own Gurkha Rifles, December 1961.

Above A cook in the Army Catering Corps preparing traditional Christmas fare in the kitchen of the British Military Hospital, Singapore, watched over by a sergeant of the Queen Alexandra's Royal Army Nursing Corps, late 1950s.

HONG KONG

Hong Kong island was ceded to Britain by China in 1842. In 1984, Britain and China signed a Joint Declaration in which it was agreed that China would resume sovereignty over Hong Kong in 1997. For more than 150 years Hong Kong was Britain's most important outpost in the Far East, representing a thriving mix of imperial ambition and Asian energy and entrepreneurship.

Right Princess Alexandra visits the fishing village of Aberdeen during her tour of Hong Kong in 1961.

Left Battery Quartermaster Sergeant Correll with his wife, family and friends in his bungalow in the army village of Sek Kong, Hong Kong, December 1957.

Above British sappers (engineers) and Chinese villagers cooperate to lay a water supply pipe to Tap Mun Chau, a small island off the east coast of Hong Kong, December 1963.

Above Sir Robert Black, governor of Hong Kong, inspecting a ceremonial guard of the 1st Battalion, Queen's Royal Surrey Regiment, February 1963. This occasion was thought to be the first time since the Second World War that soldiers in the scarlet of a full-dress British uniform had stood guard at Government House.

Left A corporal of the Middlesex Regiment being shown various landmarks in Hong Kong Harbour, *circa* 1963.

MALTA

The archipelago of Malta became part of the British Empire in 1814. It was a vitally important strategic base and managed to defend itself during the Second World War, despite massive bombardments by German and Italian aircraft. In recognition of the bravery of its people, the entire island was awarded the George Cross in 1942. Malta became independent in 1964.

Below A group of officers of the Royal Navy and the Women's Royal Naval Service (Wrens) at a drinks party overlooking the Grand Harbour at Valletta, Malta, June 1964.

GIBRALTAR

The British Crown Colony of Gibraltar, a small rocky outcrop on the south coast of Spain, was ceded to Britain by the Dutch in the Treaty of Utrecht in 1713. It has since become a very British outpost and was an important strategic base for the British Empire in its key position at the mouth of the Mediterranean.

Below Members of the Royal Air Force Sailing Club, sailing in Algeciras Bay, Gibraltar, September 1964.

CYPRUS

The island of Cyprus was leased to Britain by Turkey in 1878. Britain declared it a colony in 1925. During the 1950s, Britain became embroiled in a struggle against EOKA, a terrorist group of Greek-speaking Cypriots who were campaigning for union with mainland Greece. The island became independent in 1960 and in 1974 became a divided country with Turkish Cypriots, supported by Turkey, claiming sovereignty over 40 per cent of the island to the north. Britain still has a military presence on the island.

Below A police band performing in Nicosia, Cyprus in the 1950s.

Above Members of the Women's Royal Army Corps and the Royal Army Service Corps sightseeing in Cyprus, March 1963.

Above A Turkish refugee camp near Nicosia, Cyprus, 1964. Before partition of the island, Greeks and Turks on the wrong side of the line of demarcation between the two communities (the Green Line) had to be relocated to the other part of the island.

ADEN

When the Suez Canal opened in 1869, the seaport of Aden on the Yemeni Coast became an important base for the network of strategic ports that linked the British Empire together. Aden was made a Crown Colony in 1937 and the surrounding territory became the Aden Protectorate. Aden was granted independence in 1967, but the preceding three years were characterized by a bitter counter-insurgency campaign by British forces against Arab nationalists.

Right Private Janet Carr and Sylvia Bromwich of 28 Independent Company, Women's Royal Army Corps (WRACs) exploring Tawahi Market, Aden (March 1965).

Left Lance Corporal Meade and Private Newsome of the Army Catering Corps shopping in Aden, February 1964. The men appear to be buying toy vehicles and examining a primitive remote-controlled digger, operated by a wire.

Left A combined services patrol in Crater, Aden, March 1965. Lance Corporal Vivienne McCoy of 28 Independent Company, Women's Royal Army Corps drives leading Patrolman James Field, Royal Navy and Lance Corporal Shawn Westrip, Royal Military Police.

Right A tank in the streets of Aden in 1967. A local police mutiny during the same year led to troops of the Argyll and Sutherland Highlanders, under the command of Colin "Mad Mitch" Mitchell, occupying the Crater district of Aden to maintain order.

AFTERWORD

In 1997, Chris Patten, the last Governor of Hong Kong, bowed his head and shed a tear for the Empire. Britain's great colonial outpost in the Orient was handed over to China, as history dictated it must. Charles, Prince of Wales was there, as was the British prime minister, Tony Blair. "Auld Lang Syne" was sung, the Union flag came down and the British sailed off with dignity in the Royal Yacht *Britannia*.

But few tears were shed back home in Britain; perhaps there were some from those with strong links to the Far East and some misty eyes among those who had long memories, or were inclined to be nostalgic about Britain's imperial past. But, on the whole, the event passed as just another news report. Britain had moved on a whole generation from the great colonial handover of the 1960s and had found a new agenda, if not a new identity.

A few outposts remained; a romantic vestigial Empire, distant islands and outcrops – Bermuda (where people actually voted to remain British), Gibraltar (where people would do anything to forestall becoming Spaniards) and a few remote island communities (where most of the people seem to be descendants of the sailors who founded the Empire in the first place). One of these, the Falkland Islands, a particularly remote and inhospitable place in the South Atlantic, was (and is) coveted by its looming neighbour, Argentina. When, in a moment of madness in 1982, an unpopular military junta in Buenos Aires chose to annexe the islands by force, Britain enjoyed a splendid, if precarious, interlude of imperial adventure.

Margaret Thatcher, Britain's first female prime minister, donned the mantle of Wellington, Palmerston and Churchill and relived a glorious past. This was not a rerun of Suez – a tired old braggart trying to bully a new nation; this time Britain was secure in the belief that it had just cause. And the United States didn't intervene, but lent tacit support. The Navy steamed south in a massive armada of which Drake and Nelson would have been proud. Brave fighter pilots evoked memories of the Battle of Britain and the army and marines "yomped" heroically through the mist and bullets. It was popularly perceived as sterling stuff with the "Argies" being sent home having been taught a damned good lesson. But many thought negotiation would have been a better strategy and that British and Argentinian soldiers, sailors and airmen had died needlessly. In the end, it proved very little, except that the British had lost none of their pugilistic character and that the professional qualities of her armed forces were second to none. Indeed, in future wars, most notably in the Gulf War in 1991, and in numerous subsequent peacekeeping operations, the British soldier came to be seen as the supreme modern professional; the SAS trooper in particular became the ultimate warrior, the British "Tommy" come of age.

But the Falklands was the last hurrah. British forces are now deployed as part of a United Nations force, or within a NATO force with our north Atlantic allies, or, at best, as a competent second billing to United States forces.

In 1962, in a speech at the US military academy at West Point, the United States Secretary of State, Dean Acheson, uttered the following famous words: "Great Britain has lost an Empire, and has not yet found a role." In searching for that role, Britain has looked more and more to Europe. Perversely, the British have been preoccupied for most of their history in keeping Europe at bay and in emphasizing their differences from their neighbours. However, despite the process often being undertaken begrudgingly, Britain has become increasingly closely connected to Europe over the past four decades. The barriers are all but down, and now the "hot" political debate is not about Empire, but about whether Britain is losing its sovereignty. No wonder some are said to be turning in their imperial graves!

So what is today's legacy of Britain and her Empire? The Commonwealth continues fitfully, with almost fifty sovereign members. It doesn't do or mean much on a grand scale, but it does an enormous amount on a modest and mundane level. Ties of blood, law, education and culture stretch from the British Isles to every corner of the world in a great Anglo-Celtic diaspora. And Britain is still a major power, especially through its "special relationship" with the United States (essentially rooted in the primordial soup of "kith and kin", going back to the British settlements of America). Perhaps all formal ties with Canada, New Zealand and Australia will soon be broken, but they will always be an extension, no matter how far removed, of their British origins and the emotional tie will always remain.

And what of Britain itself? Now, although it is increasingly European, it has finally remembered – after the usefulness of the hybrid term, "British", has run its imperial course – that the nation is not a singularity, but a union of its constituent parts. The Scots, Welsh and Irish have never misplaced their identities; perhaps now the English are just beginning to remember theirs. If the new Celtic parliaments do nothing more, they may at least remind the English to say "British" when they mean the people of Great Britain and Northern Ireland, and "English" when they are referring to those people south of Hadrian's Wall and east of Offa's Dyke.

Perhaps identity is the most difficult question of all. Britain had always been a cosmopolitan community, but had managed to mould its differences into a cohesive British nation. In the postcolonial world that process has become more difficult, because large numbers of people from its former Empire have chosen Britain as a home. Prejudice and discrimination have been widespread. Riots and disturbances have followed as ethnic minorities have sought to defend and assert themselves.

The result is a new Britain: a country wedded to Europe, but a reflection of an old Empire; a multicultural society, where its indigenous population struggles to come to terms with large numbers of "foreign" arrivals from its former colonies. And in this there is a final irony. Britain is now a microcosm of its old Empire: not a global empire of ruler and ruled, but a society of equals, all sharing the mother country. Now Britain has to learn to live with it.

MODERN BRITAIN

By 1980, with the Empire becoming no more than a recent memory, Britain began to come to terms with its legacy. The most significant aspects of this legacy were twofold: first, Britain had had to accept that it was a European power, not a world power and second, the ethnic and cultural make-up of Britain had changed as a consequence of significant colonial and postcolonial population movements between Britain and its Empire.

Right Notting Hill Carnival, 1979.

Left The Notting Hill Carnival, 1979. The carnival, a celebration of Caribbean culture in Britain, began in 1964. Often a focus for tension, Notting Hill saw Britain's first racial disturbances in 1958. Race riots in Britain in the 1980s, in places like Brixton, London, St Pauls, Bristol and Toxteth, Liverpool, demonstrated the fragility of multicultural Britain. In the late 1990s, trouble began to flare up in northern towns and cities with significant Asian communities.

Above Notting Hill Carnival, 1979.

ROAD TO EQUALITY

Despite numerous problems, Britain has slowly adapted to the end of the Empire during the last thirty years. The Commission for Racial Equality and strong legislation against discrimination have helped to alleviate many of the problems of racism in Britain. However, barriers still persist in many areas of employment, like the armed forces, the police and the law. Areas like sport, entertainment, fashion and the media appear to be more meritocratic.

Above Bengali housing, Peel Square, Bradford. A large Asian communities grew up in Bradford after the Second World War, particularly in the late 1950s and 1960s.

Right Manningham Middle School, Bradford, founded in 1971, taught a very cosmopolitan mix of children from the West Indies, Pakistan, Bangladesh, India, China, Fiji and Uganda; all former British colonies.

Right A scene which seems to bring round into a full circle 250 years of British imperial history: British Asians wearing traditional costumes in Lister Park, Bradford.

INDEX

Note: Page numbers in *italics* refer to caption information.

PICTURE CREDITS